LEADERSHIP STYLE TO SUCCESSFUL HOSPITALITY AND TOURISM MANAGEMENT

BY

Agbebi Pius A. (FHATMAN, PhD)

1

PREFACE

Effective and more focused leadership is paramount in navigating the complex and dynamic landscape of hospitality and tourism management in the whole continents. This preface sets the stage for exploring diverse leadership styles that contribute to success in this ever-evolving industry. From visionary approaches that shape the future of hospitality to adaptive styles that respond to the nuanced demands of tourism, the pages ahead delve into the essential qualities and strategies that empower leaders to excel in guiding teams and organizations within this vibrant sector. As we embark on this exploration, the goal is to illuminate the multifaceted nature of leadership and its integral role in achieving excellence in hospitality and tourism management. Thus, this book will provide all managers and supervisors in the hospitality and tourism industry the necessary and pertinent ideas to successfully steer the ship of the industry to the desired goals of sustainable growth and development.

Agbebi Pius A. (FHATMAN, PhD)

TABLE OF CONTENTS

1.0   Introduction

1.1 Overview of Hospitality and Tourism industry

The Hospitality and Tourism industry encompasses various sectors, including lodging, food and beverage, transportation, entertainment, and travel services. It revolves around providing services to people who are away from their homes for leisure, business, or other purposes. This industry plays a crucial role in global economies, creating employment opportunities and contributing significantly to Gross Domestic Product. Key components include hotels, restaurants, airlines, travel agencies, and attractions, all working together to offer enjoyable and convenient experiences for travelers.

1.2 Importance of leadership in the Hospitality and Tourism sector

Leadership in the Hospitality and Tourism sector is crucial for several reasons. Firstly, it sets the tone for customer service, influencing staff to prioritize guest satisfaction. Effective leaders inspire and motivate teams to deliver exceptional experiences, which is essential in an industry heavily dependent on customer perceptions.

Secondly, in a sector known for its dynamic nature and diverse workforce, strong leadership fosters adaptability and innovation. Leaders navigate through challenges such as changing market trends, technological advancements, and evolving consumer preferences, ensuring the business stays competitive.

Moreover, leaders play a vital role in creating a positive work culture. A motivated and well-led team is more likely to provide superior service, leading to customer loyalty and positive reviews.

In summary, leadership is integral in shaping organizational culture, driving innovation, and ensuring high-quality service delivery, all of which contribute to the success of businesses in the Hospitality and Tourism sector.

2.0 Leadership Style

1. Collaborative leadership

2. Servant leadership

3. Transformational leadership

Collaborative leadership involves fostering a team-oriented approach where leaders and team members work together to achieve common goals. It emphasizes open communication, shared decision-making, and leveraging the diverse strengths within the team. This style aims to harness collective intelligence and create an inclusive environment where everyone's input is valued. Collaboration promotes innovation, adaptability, and a sense of ownership among team members.

Servant leadership is characterized by a leader's focus on serving and prioritizing the needs of others, putting the team's well-being above personal gain. Such leaders actively listen, empathize, and support their team members. They aim to nurture personal and professional growth within the team, fostering a culture of collaboration and mutual respect. Servant leaders often lead by example, embodying the values they expect from their team.

Transformational leadership involves inspiring and motivating followers to achieve exceptional results and personal growth. Leaders employing this style often have a clear vision, charisma, and the ability to articulate a compelling future. They encourage creativity and innovation, challenging the status quo to drive positive change. Transformational leaders build strong relationships with their team, fostering a sense of trust and loyalty. Their influence goes beyond mere transactions, transforming the organizational culture and inspiring higher performance.

Each leadership style has its unique strengths, and the effectiveness depends on the context and organizational needs.

3.0 Impact of leadership on Productivity and Profitability in Hospitality and tourism Industry

Leadership has a profound impact on productivity within an organization. Here are key ways in which leadership influences productivity:

1. Motivation and Morale
Effective leaders inspire and motivate their teams, creating a positive work environment. When employees feel valued and motivated, they are more likely to be engaged and productive. Positive morale contributes to a sense of purpose and commitment, leading to increased effort and output.

2. Communication and Clarity

Clear communication from leadership ensures that team members understand their roles, goals, and expectations. Ambiguity or confusion can hinder productivity. Leaders who communicate effectively reduce misunderstandings, enabling the team to focus on tasks without unnecessary disruptions.

3. Empowerment and Autonomy

Empowering employees with decision-making authority and autonomy can boost productivity. Trusting team members to take ownership of their work fosters a sense of responsibility and accountability, encouraging them to perform at their best.

4. Adaptability and Innovation

Leaders who encourage innovation and adaptability contribute to increased productivity. Embracing new ideas and processes allows teams to find more efficient ways of working, leading to improved productivity over time.

5. Conflict Resolution

Skilled leaders address conflicts promptly and constructively. Resolving issues within the team prevents productivity losses due to tension or disruption. Leaders who foster a collaborative and supportive atmosphere minimize the negative impact of conflicts on overall productivity.

6. Resource Allocation

Effective leaders ensure that resources, including time and personnel, are allocated efficiently. Proper planning and allocation prevent bottlenecks, optimize workflows, and contribute to sustained high productivity.

In summary, leadership influences productivity by creating a positive work culture, facilitating effective communication, empowering and motivating team members, fostering innovation, resolving conflicts, and ensuring efficient resource utilization. The impact of leadership on productivity is multifaceted and plays a crucial role in the overall success of an organization.

4.0 Case Study: Marriott International

4.1 Background

Marriott International is a global hospitality company known for its diverse portfolio of hotels and resorts. Arne Sorenson served as the CEO of Marriott from 2012 until his passing in 2021, leaving a significant legacy in the industry.

4.2 Leadership Practices

(i) Global Expansion and Brand Diversification
Under Sorenson's leadership, Marriott pursued strategic global expansion and diversified its brand portfolio. The acquisition of Starwood Hotels in 2016 expanded Marriott's reach, making it the largest hotel company globally. This bold move showcased Sorenson's visionary leadership in navigating the competitive landscape.

(ii) Focus on Technology and Innovation

Sorenson embraced technology to enhance customer experience. The introduction of the Marriott Bonvoy loyalty program, mobile check-in, and digital concierge services reflected a commitment to innovation. These initiatives not only improved customer satisfaction but also streamlined operations for increased efficiency.

(iii) Commitment to Diversity and Inclusion
Marriott prioritized diversity and inclusion under Sorenson's leadership. The company aimed to create an inclusive work environment and implemented programs to support minority-owned businesses. Sorenson's commitment to diversity not only resonated with social responsibility but also positively impacted the company's reputation.

(iv) Environmental Sustainability
Sorenson recognized the importance of environmental sustainability in the hospitality industry. Marriott

implemented initiatives to reduce its environmental footprint, such as energy-efficient buildings and responsible sourcing practices. This commitment to sustainability aligned with changing consumer expectations and demonstrated Marriott's corporate responsibility.

(v) Crisis Management during COVID-19

Sorenson faced unprecedented challenges during the COVID-19 pandemic. His transparent and empathetic communication with employees, customers, and investors showcased strong crisis management. Marriott implemented flexible cancellation policies, supported furloughed employees, and adapted operations to ensure safety, reflecting Sorenson's people-centric approach.

4.3 Results

Marriott International, under Arne Sorenson's leadership, experienced significant growth, becoming a global hospitality giant. The company's emphasis on technology, sustainability, diversity, and crisis management contributed to its success and resilience. Sorenson's legacy is marked by a commitment to innovation, social responsibility, and a customer-centric approach, setting a benchmark for leadership practices in the Hospitality and Tourism industry.

4.4 Challenges

(i) Global Economic Uncertainties
Challenge: The hospitality industry is susceptible to economic fluctuations and global uncertainties, impacting travel and tourism.

Solution: Implement strategic financial planning, diversify revenue streams, and maintain a flexible business model to adapt to economic changes.

(ii) Technology Disruptions
Challenge: Rapid advancements in technology require continuous adaptation to stay competitive.

Solution: Invest in innovative technologies, regularly update systems, and provide ongoing training to employees to ensure they can leverage new tools effectively.

(3) Talent Retention and Development
Challenge: The industry faces challenges in attracting and retaining skilled employees, especially in diverse global markets.

Solution: Implement comprehensive talent development programs, offer competitive compensation, and foster a positive work culture to attract and retain top talent.

(4) Environmental Sustainability Pressures
Challenge: Increasing environmental concerns and regulations pose challenges for sustainable practices in the hospitality sector.

Solution: Continue investing in sustainable initiatives, such as energy-efficient technologies, waste reduction programs, and eco-friendly practices, to align with changing consumer preferences.

(5) Competitive Landscape

Challenge: Intense competition in the hospitality industry requires ongoing differentiation to stand out.

Solution: Regularly assess market trends, innovate services and amenities, and maintain a strong brand identity to remain competitive.

4.5 Solutions

(i) Strategic Partnerships

Collaborate with strategic partners to enhance offerings, share resources, and expand market reach. This can help Marriott navigate economic uncertainties and strengthen its position in the industry.

(ii) Investment in Employee Training

Prioritize ongoing training programs for employees to adapt to technological changes. This ensures that staff can deliver high-quality service, and it aligns with Marriott's commitment to innovation.

(iii) Diversity and Inclusion Initiatives

Continue and expand diversity and inclusion initiatives to attract a diverse workforce. Embracing a multicultural approach can enhance the overall guest experience and contribute to the company's success in global markets.

(iv) Innovation Hubs and Research

Establish innovation hubs to stay ahead of technological trends. Investing in research and development allows Marriott to anticipate and implement cutting-edge technologies, maintaining a competitive edge in the market.

(v) Community Engagement and Sustainability Programs

Strengthen community engagement and sustainability programs to showcase Marriott's commitment to responsible business practices. This can enhance the brand's reputation and appeal to environmentally conscious consumers.

By addressing these challenges with strategic solutions, Marriott can continue to uphold successful leadership practices, ensuring sustained growth and resilience in the dynamic Hospitality and Tourism industry.

5.0 Strategies for Effective Leadership

Effective leadership involves implementing various strategies to guide teams, foster a positive work environment, and achieve organizational goals. Here are key strategies for effective leadership:

(i) Visionary Leadership
Define a clear and inspiring vision for the organization. A compelling vision provides direction and purpose, motivating the team to work towards common goals.

(ii) Lead by Example

Demonstrate the values and behaviors expected from the team. Leading by example fosters trust, credibility, and a strong work ethic among team members.

(iii) Effective Communication

Establish open and transparent communication channels. Regularly share information, provide feedback, and actively listen to the concerns and ideas of team members. Clarity in communication prevents misunderstandings and aligns everyone with organizational objectives.

(iv) Empowerment and Delegation

Empower team members by delegating responsibilities and decision-making authority. Trusting your team fosters a sense of ownership, boosts morale, and allows individuals to showcase their skills and talents.

(v) Adaptability and Flexibility

Navigate through change with resilience and adaptability. A leader who embraces change and guides the team through challenges helps create a dynamic and responsive organization.

(vi)Team Building and Collaboration
Foster a collaborative and inclusive team culture. Encourage cooperation, celebrate diversity, and build strong interpersonal relationships to enhance teamwork and productivity.

(vii) Strategic Thinking

Develop a strategic mindset to anticipate challenges and opportunities. Effective leaders analyze situations, make informed decisions, and align actions with long-term organizational goals.

(viii) Continuous Learning
Embrace a commitment to lifelong learning. Stay updated on industry trends, new technologies, and leadership best practices. A leader's willingness to learn sets a positive example for the team.

(ix) Recognition and Appreciation

Acknowledge and appreciate the efforts and achievements of team members. Regular recognition boosts morale, reinforces positive behavior, and creates a motivated and engaged workforce.

(x) Conflict Resolution

Address conflicts promptly and constructively. A leader skilled in conflict resolution can maintain a harmonious work environment and prevent interpersonal issues from affecting productivity.

(xi) Ethical Leadership

Uphold ethical standards and integrity in decision-making. Ethical leadership builds trust, both within the team and with stakeholders, contributing to the long-term success and reputation of the organization.

(xii) Results-Oriented Focus

Set clear performance expectations and key performance indicators. Focus on achieving measurable results and celebrate milestones to keep the team motivated and aligned with organizational objectives.

Combining these strategies creates a comprehensive approach to effective leadership, fostering a positive organizational culture and driving success in the long run.

6.0   Conclusion

6.1 A restatement of key findings on Leadership Style and Productivity in Hospitality and Tourism business.

(i) People-Centric Leadership is Vital

In the Hospitality and Tourism industry, leadership styles that prioritize employee satisfaction and motivation tend to correlate with higher productivity. This sector heavily relies on customer service, and happy, engaged employees are more likely to deliver exceptional service, positively impacting productivity.

(ii) Adaptability is a Key Leadership Trait

The dynamic nature of the industry requires leaders to be adaptable. Those who can navigate unexpected challenges, such as changing travel trends or global events, tend to maintain higher productivity levels. This adaptability often aligns with a transformational leadership style.

(iii) Innovation and Technology Integration

Successful leaders in this sector embrace innovation, incorporating technology to enhance guest experiences and streamline operations. A leadership style that encourages a tech-savvy approach and continuous improvement tends to boost efficiency and productivity.

(iv) Collaborative Leadership Enhances Team Performance

Given the diverse and often cross-functional nature of tasks in hospitality and tourism, leaders who adopt a collaborative approach, encouraging teamwork and open communication, often see improved productivity. This collaborative leadership style helps in problem-solving and ensures a cohesive working environment.

(v) Employee Training and Development Impact Service Quality

Leaders who invest in ongoing training and development for their teams contribute to enhanced service quality.

Well-trained staff members are more confident and competent, positively affecting customer satisfaction and, subsequently, productivity.

(vi) Strategic Vision and Planning are Crucial

Effective leaders in this industry demonstrate strategic vision and planning. Those who can anticipate industry trends, plan for peak seasons, and make informed decisions tend to steer their organizations towards sustained productivity.

(vii) Crisis Management and Resilience

The ability to effectively manage crises, such as natural disasters or global health emergencies, is a distinguishing factor. Leaders who demonstrate resilience and guide their teams through challenging times contribute to maintaining productivity levels even in adverse conditions.

It's important to note that the hospitality and tourism sector is subject to external factors like economic conditions, geopolitical events, and public health crises. Effective leadership not only focuses on day-to-day operations but also equips organizations to navigate these external challenges, safeguarding productivity and ensuring long-term success.

6.2 Future trends of Leadership Style and Productivity in Hospitality and tourism

General trends that were shaping leadership styles and productivity in the Hospitality and Tourism industry. Keep in mind that the industry is dynamic, and new trends may have emerged since then. Here are some anticipated future trends:

1. Technology Integration

Leaders in the hospitality sector are expected to increasingly leverage technology for enhanced guest experiences and streamlined operations. This includes the use of artificial intelligence, data analytics, and smart technologies to personalize services and optimize efficiency.

2. Emphasis on Sustainability

The future will likely see a continued focus on sustainable practices. Leaders are expected to adopt eco-friendly initiatives, reduce carbon footprints, and emphasize responsible tourism to align with growing consumer preferences for environmentally conscious travel.

3. Remote and Flexible Work
The COVID-19 pandemic accelerated remote work trends across industries. While the nature of the hospitality industry requires on-site staff, leadership may explore flexible work arrangements for roles that can accommodate remote work, contributing to employee satisfaction and potentially improving productivity.

4. Customer-Centric Leadership
With increasing competition and the importance of customer loyalty, leaders will likely continue to adopt customer-centric leadership styles. This involves a deep

understanding of customer needs, preferences, and the ability to align organizational strategies with evolving customer expectations.

5. Focus on Employee Well-being

Future leaders in hospitality are expected to prioritize employee well-being. This includes mental health support, work-life balance initiatives, and fostering a positive workplace culture. A happy and healthy workforce is likely to contribute to higher productivity.

6. Adaptive Leadership for Crisis Management

Given the unpredictability of external events, leaders will need to further enhance their adaptive leadership skills. The ability to navigate crises, such as pandemics or geopolitical challenges, will be crucial for maintaining productivity and sustaining business operations.

7. Continuous Learning and Up-skilling:

The rapid evolution of technology and changing consumer behaviors will require leaders and employees to engage in continuous learning. Leaders who promote a culture of learning and invest in up-skilling their teams are likely to stay ahead of industry trends and enhance productivity.

8. Innovative Guest Experiences

Leaders will need to foster a culture of innovation to create unique and memorable guest experiences. This may involve incorporating augmented reality, virtual reality, and other immersive technologies to enhance the overall hospitality experience.

9. Diversity, Equity, and Inclusion (DEI)

The focus on diversity, equity, and inclusion is expected to continue. Leaders who prioritize DEI initiatives are likely to build more inclusive work environments, fostering creativity and collaboration, ultimately contributing to increased productivity.

It's important for leaders in the hospitality and tourism industry to stay attuned to emerging trends, adapt their leadership styles accordingly, and embrace innovative strategies to drive productivity in this ever-evolving landscape.

Bibliography/references

1. Kim, H.J *et al* (2011). Hospitality service employees' coping style: the role of emotional intelligence, two basic personalities. *International Journal of Hospitality Management, vol30, issue 3*. Page Retrieved on 2nd January, 2024 from: https://doi.org/10.1016/j.ijhm.

2. Irene, H.V *et al* (2019). 'Effects of different leadership styles on hospitality workers'. Journal of tourism management. Vol.71, pgs., 402-420. Retrieved 2nd January, 2024 from: https://doi.org/10.1016/j.tourman.

3. Giang, H; Minigun Y; N Tuan T.L (2023). Ethical leadership in tourism and hospitality management: A systematic literature review and research agenda. International journal of hospitality management Vol.114, pgs. 103-563.

Retrieved 2nd January, 2024 from:
https://doi.org./10.1016/j.ijhm.

4. Marriott International (2023). Marriott
    Leadership: An overview research. Retrieved on
    10th January, 2024 from:
    https://research.methodology.net

5. Philip, K. (2019). Leadership and Public good.
    Retrieved on 10th January, 2024 from:
    https://www.marketingjournal .

6. Peter, D. (2019). What is leadership Style?
    Retrieved on 11th January, 2024 from:
    https://www.coperatelearningnetwork.com.